A Kid's Guide
to the
Classification
of
Living Things™

Plants Without Seeds

Elaine Pascoe

Photographs by Dwight Kuhn

The Rosen Publishing Group's
PowerKids Press™
New York

Published in 2003 by The Rosen Publishing Group, Inc.
29 East 21st Street, New York, NY 10010

First Edition

Editor: Natashya Wilson
Book Design: Emily Muschinske

Photo Credits: All photographs © Dwight Kuhn

Pascoe, Elaine.
Plants without seeds / Elaine Pascoe ; photography by Dwight Kuhn.—
1st ed.
    p. cm. — (A kid's guide to the classification of living things) Summary: An introduction to the life cycles and characteristics of bryophytes, or plants without seeds, such as mosses and ferns.
Includes bibliographical references (p.   ).
  ISBN 0-8239-6315-2
1. Cryptogams—Juvenile literature. [1. Cryptogams.] I. Kuhn, Dwight, ill. II. Title.
  QK505.5 .P37 2003
  586—dc21
                                                                              2001007794

Manufactured in the United States of America

Contents

Kingdoms of Living Things

A patch of soft, green moss grows beneath a big oak tree. The moss and the oak do not seem much alike. Where does each belong in the family of living things?

To answer questions like this, scientists compare living things. They look closely at all the ways in which one living thing is like another, and all the ways in which each is different. Then the living things are sorted into groups, based on the ways in which they are alike. This is called classification.

Most scientists group living things into five **kingdoms**. Each kingdom is then sorted into smaller and smaller groups. This book is about some members of the plant kingdom, plants without seeds.

The plant kingdom can be sorted into plants with and without seeds. In the diagram, the plants-without-seeds group is sorted into smaller groups.

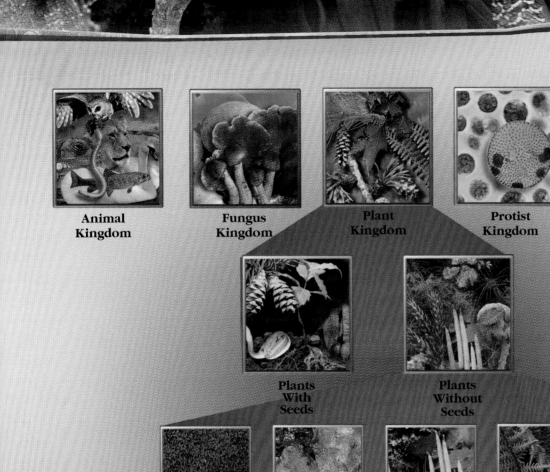

Animal Kingdom

Fungus Kingdom

Plant Kingdom

Protist Kingdom

Monera Kingdom

Plants With Seeds

Plants Without Seeds

Mosses

Liverworts

Club Mosses

Ferns

Horsetails

Tree Club Moss

Stiff Club Moss

Runners Pine

Seedless Plants

How are plants different from animals? A plant grows in one place, but an animal moves around. Plants make their own food. Animals do not. Plants have materials called **pigments**, which help them to make food through a process called **photosynthesis**. **Chlorophyll**, the most common pigment, is green.

Some of the plants you know best, such as grass and trees, make seeds. That is how they **reproduce**, or multiply. Other plants do not make seeds. These seedless plants include mosses, liverworts, club mosses, ferns, and horsetails. They reproduce by forming **spores**. Spores are often kept in small, bumpy cases on these plants' leaves or stems.

Many different kinds, or species, of mosses are growing on and around this fallen tree.

Mosses: Green Cushions

Mosses are simple plants. They do not have true roots, stems, and leaves. In other plants, the roots take up water and other **nutrients** from the soil. The simple plants draw water and nutrients right into their green plant parts.

Mosses grow under trees, on the banks of streams, and in other damp and shady places. There are thousands of different kinds of mosses. Most form carpets of little plants packed closely together. A patch of moss can feel soft, like a cushion or a pile of feathers. These little plants are tough, however. They can be found on cold mountain peaks and in other places where most plants cannot grow.

Mosses do not have true roots. This makes it easy for mosses to grow on rocks. Plants with true roots must grow where there is soil.

9

Mosses: Making Spores

Moss plants have male and female shoots. The male shoots make male reproductive **cells**, and the female shoots make female reproductive cells, called **egg cells**. The male and female cells must get together for spores to form. For that to happen, moss plants need water. When moss is wet, the male cells swim to the female shoots to find the female cells. The male cells have whiplike tails called **flagella**, which they wiggle to move through the water.

When the male and female cells join, a spore case begins to form. In most mosses, the case is carried on a thin stalk. Inside are millions of tiny spores. The spore case opens, and the wind carries away the spores. Each spore can grow into a new plant.

 This moss spore case, at the top of the thin, red stalk, is releasing spores. New moss might grow wherever the spores land.

A young red-spotted newt crawls across a soft, green carpet of moss.

This moss has formed spore cases. The spores inside will grow into new moss after they are released.

When the male and the female cells join, a spore case such as this one forms.

When the moss's spore case is full of spores, it opens to let out the spores. The spores float away on the wind.

Liverworts

As mosses are, liverworts are simple plants. They do not have true stems, roots, or leaves.

There are several kinds of liverworts. One common kind looks a lot like a small piece of lettuce. The plant's body is flat and grows close to the ground. These little plants are found along streams, on rocks and tree trunks, and in other damp, shady places.

Scientists have found **fossils** of liverworts that are almost 400 million years old. Liverworts may have been the first plants to live on land.

This liverwort shows the lettucelike look typical of many of these simple plants.

Liverworts got their name because they were once thought to help cure illnesses of the liver. "Wort" comes from an Old-English word for "herb."

When you spot a liverwort, you might think you've spotted a salad growing on the ground.

Club Mosses

Club mosses look like mosses, but a close look shows that they are different. These plants have roots, stems, and leaves. The roots grow down into the soil and soak up water and other nutrients. Water and nutrients travel up the stem to the tiny leaves, which cover the stem. Each leaf has only one vein to carry the water and nutrients.

Club mosses grow throughout the world. One kind of club moss can grow under ice and snow. Others grow in tropical rain forests. In northern forests, club mosses grow in many of the same areas as mosses. Some common club mosses look like tiny fir trees. They carry their spores on candlelike shoots.

The candlelike shoots on this ground-pine club moss carry its spores.

Ferns: Feathery Leaves

Ferns are seedless plants with roots, stems, and beautiful, feathery leaves. There are thousands of different kinds of ferns. In tropical forests, some ferns grow to be 65 feet (20 m) high. In forests in cooler places, ferns can grow to be 3 feet (1 m) tall, but most are smaller. The leaves of these ferns die when cold weather comes in fall. The roots and stems stay alive underground. In spring new leaves push up out of the ground. The new leaves are curled up. They are called **fiddleheads** because they are shaped like the curved head of a violin. The leaves gradually uncurl and grow. Each leaf is made of many small leaflets growing from a central stem.

When you see a group of plants shaped like the top ends of violins, you know you are looking at newly growing ferns.

Club mosses can be found growing alongside other plants, such as lichens and mosses.

These club moss shoots are giving off the club moss's spores. New club mosses can grow wherever they land.

As do many fir trees, many club mosses stay green year-round.

Fern leaves can live from 1 to 2 years. The roots and stems can live for 100 years!

When they are ready to reproduce, some ferns form spores on stalks.

Ferns: How New Ferns Grow

Ferns form spores, as do all seedless plants. Some ferns carry their spores on tall stalks. Others carry the spores under their leaves or on their stems. Wind carries away the spores.

If a spore lands in a place with good growing conditions, a new plant grows. This plant does not look like the fern that made the spores. It is tiny, with one heart-shaped leaf. The little plant is called a **prothallus**, which means "first growth." It makes male and female reproductive cells. When a male and a female cell join, the little plant grows into a fern. The fern will make more spores, beginning the cycle again.

This type of fern, a crested fern, carries its spores in brown cases under its leaves, as shown here. Inset: *This fiddlehead will soon uncurl its leaves.*

Horsetails

Horsetails are seedless plants with hollow, jointed stems. About 300 million years ago, there were forests of giant horsetails the size of trees. Today most members of this plant group grow no more than about 3 feet (1 m) tall.

A horsetail's stem grows along the ground, just under the surface. Roots grow into the ground. Shoots grow up into the air. The horsetail has two kinds of shoots. Spore-making shoots are pale tan or brown. Green shoots have branching stems covered with tiny scales. The scales are the plant's leaves. The green shoots look a bit like a horse's tail, and that is how this plant got its name.

These are the tan and brown spore-making shoots of a horsetail plant.

1

This is the prothallus of a fern. It will start to grow into a fern when the male and the female reproductive cells join.

Once the male and the female cells join, the fern begins to grow.

2

3

The full-grown ferns are green and leafy.

Soon they form spores, either on stalks such as this one, or in cases on the stems or under the leaves.

4

Horsetail plant shoots grow from the plant's stem, which stretches out just below the ground.

When you see tall stems with bristly, hairlike leaves such as these, you know you are looking at horsetail plants.

What Living Things Share

A carpet of moss covers the bank of a stream. In the water, a fish swims by. The moss and the fish do not seem much alike, but they have a lot in common with each other and with all living things.

As do all living things, they reproduce. Moss plants make new moss plants. Fish lay eggs that hatch into new fish. They also grow, and they need food. Plants make their food. Other living things get food in many ways. All living things sense the world around them and react to it.

The Sun helps to make life possible, but it is not a living thing. It does not eat, and it doesn't make more suns.

Nonliving things have none of these traits. Fake plants do not grow. Stuffed animals do not eat. This book cannot make more books. In these ways, nonliving things are different from living things.

Glossary

cells (SELZ) Tiny units that make up all living things.

chlorophyll (KLOR-uh-fil) A green pigment that allows plants to use energy from sunlight to make food.

egg cells (EHG SELZ) Female reproductive cells.

fiddleheads (FIH-dul-hedz) New fern leaves, before they uncurl.

flagella (fluh-JEH-luh) Wiggling, tail-like structures.

fossils (FAH-sulz) Remains left by plants and animals that lived millions of years ago.

kingdoms (KING-duhmz) The five major divisions of living things.

nutrients (NOO-tree-ints) Anything that a living thing needs to live and grow.

photosynthesis (foh-toh-SIN-thuh-sis) The process in which leaves use energy from sunlight, gases from air, and water from soil to make food and release oxygen.

pigments (PIG-mehntz) Materials that give color and have a variety of roles inside cells.

prothallus (proh-THA-lus) A tiny plant, or "first growth," that is a step in the reproduction of ferns.

reproduce (ree-pruh-DOOS) To make more of something.

spores (SPORZ) Special cells that can grow into a new organism, such as a plant.

Index

Web Sites

Due to the changing nature of Internet links, PowerKids Press has developed an online list of Web sites related to the subject of this book. This site is updated regularly. Please use this link to access the list:

www.powerkidslinks.com/kgclt/plwoseed/